ALBERT RECKITT ARCHAEOLOGICAL TRUST LECTURE

THE STUDY OF WINCHESTER: ARCHAEOLOGY AND HISTORY IN A BRITISH TOWN, 1961-1983

By MARTIN BIDDLE

Read 9 March 1983

I

It was Time and Chance, as Dame Joan Evans, the first benefactor of our work, would have said, which led to the start of renewed excavations in Winchester in 1961. Two years before, in his pioneering discussion of 'Winchester Cathedral in the tenth century', Mr Roger Quirk, CB, had set out for the first time the evidence relating to the sites of the Old and New Minsters, and had concluded with a plea for their excavation.[1] In 1960, when working on his second paper dealing with 'Winchester New Minster and its tenth-century tower',[2] Quirk realized that the site then proposed for a new hotel (now The Wessex Hotel), in the centre of Winchester, was precisely that (as he then believed)[3] of the New Minster church itself. Utilizing to the full his knowledge both of the local scene (he was a Wykehamist) and of the Civil Service (in which he was an Under Secretary), Quirk moved rapidly to secure the excavation of the site. With the whole-hearted co-operation of Messrs. Trust Houses Ltd., the Winchester City Council, and the then Ministry of Works, permission was granted and funds were obtained. The Society of Antiquaries, asked to nominate a director, suggested your speaker today, who was then in his final year as an undergraduate at Cambridge.

[1] R. N. Quirk, 'Winchester Cathedral in the Tenth Century', *Archaeological Journal*, 114 (1957), 28-68 (published Jan. 1959), see esp. pp. 64-8 and fig. 1.

[2] Quirk, 'Winchester New Minister and its Tenth-century Tower', *Journal of the British Archaeological Association*, 3rd. ser. 24 (1961), 16-54.

[3] Ibid., pp. 49-54, fig. 6. Quirk revised his views on the site of New Minster in Martin Biddle and R. N. Quirk, 'Excavations near Winchester Cathedral, 1961', *Archaeological Journal*, 119 (1962), 150-94 (= I. Interim: for a list, see below, Appendix A), see esp. pp. 173-82, and fig. 6. The matter was finally settled in 1963 by the discovery of 'Building G' and its identification as New Minster (II. Interim, pp. 210-11, fig. 5; cf. III. Interim, p. 257, fig. 4).

The excavation which followed showed something of the potential of Winchester's buried past. A major public building, probably the forum, a street, and a large town house of the Roman period were overlain by an extensive complex of buildings of several periods related to the New Minster monastery.[1] But the excavation was more important for what it began, for it was impossible in those days to work a long summer in Winchester and not to realize the untapped wealth of the city's archaeology, and the extent to which it was threatened with elimination through the demands of modern development. Building on Quirk's vision of an investigation of the Anglo-Saxon minsters, a broader plan of urban research was conceived and the following spring the Winchester Excavations Committee was formed with this in mind.[2] The chairman from the start was Mrs E. C. Neate, OBE, FSA, who has remained to this day, and to whom much of the success of our work is due.

Such was the *ad hoc* origin of the work of the Committee and its child, the Winchester Research Unit. There had been a number of previous committees of this kind, most recently the Roman and Medieval London Excavation Council,[3] the Canterbury Archaeological Committee, the Cirencester Excavation Committee, and the Verulamium Excavation Committee, but a comparable body founded in Winchester in 1954 was moribund by 1960. Archaeological work in the city had begun in 1949 and between then and 1960 many sites were excavated or recorded during development. The credit for this belongs entirely to the then curator of the Winchester City Museums, Mr Frank Cotrill, FSA, to the City Council, and to the then town clerk, Mr R. H. McCall, CBE. The results of this early work are being published by the City Council in a series of volumes now edited by Dr John Collis, FSA, under the title *Winchester Excavations 1949-60*.[4]

[1] I. Interim.

[2] I. Interim, p. 150; cf. II. Interim, p. 188 and Winchester Studies (for a list, see below, Appendix B), 1, p. vii.

[3] For the origins of the Council, see W. F. Grimes, *The Excavation of Roman and Medieval London* (London, 1968), pp. 1-2, 218-23, 242-51 and the remarks in Martin Biddle and Daphne Hudson, *The Future of London's Past* (Worcester, 1973), pp. 5-7.

[4] Barry Cunliffe, *Winchester Excavations 1949-60*, 1 (Winchester, 1964), dealt mainly with sites within the walls; John Collis, *Winchester Excavations 1949-60*, 2 (Winchester, 1978), with excavations in the suburbs. Volume 3, now in proof, will deal with excavations in St George's Street and High Street (except for those described in Volume 1). Volume 4 will be devoted to the remaining sites of 1949-60 and Volume 5 will deal with post-medieval pottery and other finds. For the history and nature of the work of 1949-60, see Vol. 1, pp. iii-v and Vol. 2, pp. xv-xvi, 1-3.

These excavations carried out up to 1960 were, however, too limited both in scale and approach to make any real impact at the time on the study of Winchester as an urban community. Even the investigation of Roman Winchester (*Venta Belgarum*), which was the focus of much of this work, did not make the advances which were being made in the fifties in a number of other towns of Roman origin.

To a great extent Winchester in 1961 was still *terra incognita*. Nothing certain was known of its origins, almost nothing of its street plan in Roman times, a little of its Roman defences,[1] much less of its cemeteries. As for Winchester after the Romans, it did not even exist as an organized field of archaeological enquiry, except for a few church sites and a large number of pits of every kind containing pottery and other objects which were a rich source for some of the late Dr G. C. Dunning's pioneering studies.[2]

In all this the archaeology of Winchester was little different then from that of most other towns in Britain.[3] But the very contrast between the historical evidence for the importance of early medieval Winchester and the virtual absence of an archaeology of that period, to say nothing of the preceding and following periods, compelled attention.

From the moment of its foundation in 1962, the objectives and approaches of the work of the Winchester Excavations Committee were clearly defined. The city was then passing through a period of intensive rebuilding and development which offered many opportunities for archaeological research. The Assize Courts were to be rebuilt, the offices of the Hampshire County Council greatly extended, some twenty-nine acres of the Brooks area were to be redeveloped and an inner ring road was in the offing. The Second Interim Report, dealing with the Committee's first two seasons in 1962-3, set out the attitudes which were to guide its work:

With these opportunities in view, the committee was formed to undertake excavations, both in advance of building projects, and on sites not so threatened, aimed at studying the development of Winchester as a town from its earliest origins to the establishment of the

[1] But see Barry Cunliffe, 'The Winchester City Wall', *Proceedings of the Hampshire Field Club*, 22 (2) (1962), 51–81, esp. pp. 79–81.

[2] For studies dealing specifically with finds from Winchester, see the bibliography of Dunning's publications in V. I. Evison, H. Hodges, and J. G. Hurst (eds.), *Medieval Pottery from Excavations: Studies presented to Gerald Clough Dunning* (London, 1974), pp. 17–32, items 141, 179, 202, 207–9, 278.

[3] See my comments on the situation, 'Archaeology and the History of British Towns', *Antiquity*, 42 (1968), 109–116 with the rejoinders ibid. 43 (1969), 42–3.

modern city. The centre of interest is the city itself, not any one period of its past, nor any one part of its remains. But we can hope that this approach will in particular throw light upon the end of the Roman city and on the establishment and development of the Saxon town, problems as vital to our understanding of urban development in this country, as they are difficult to solve. Further it is essential to this approach that the study and interpretation of the documentary evidence should go hand in hand with archaeological research, . . .[1]

By the next season in 1964 the collection and use of evidence derived from a wide range of the natural sciences had been explicitly incorporated in the framework of the project,[2] partly in response to the then still astonishing preservation of organic material in the waterlogged deposits of the Brooks area, partly as the natural result of a Cambridge training under the influence of the Second Albert Reckitt Archaeological Lecturer, Professor Grahame Clark, FBA.[3]

Looking back now over two decades at these aims and approaches, what strikes me is how well they have stood up to the passage of time. They only need translation to appear quite modern: the research strategy was innovative, multidisciplinary, diachronic. In other ways the basic attitudes are perhaps even today ahead of their time: the chance opportunities offered by threatened sites were to be grasped, but were not to become a strait-jacket. 'Rescue' was always subordinate to research, a policy which involved both the excavation of unthreatened sites, and the refusal to excavate threatened sites simply because they were there. All rescue was research, but not all research was rescue.[4] The unifying theme was the urban phenomenon through time and the raw material everything which was potentially grist to this mill. Selection—today we might say sampling—was the key in reducing to manageable proportions the imbalance between the extraordinary potential of Winchester's archaeology and the relatively limited resources available to deal with it.

[1] II. Interim, p. 188.

[2] III. Interim, pp. 245-6; cf. IV. Interim, pp. 318-19. See also Martin Biddle, 'Winchester: the Archaeology of a City', *Science Journal*, Mar. 1965, pp. 55-61, esp. p. 61; and Alan W. Pike and Martin Biddle, 'Parasite Eggs in Medieval Winchester', *Antiquity*, 40 (1966), 243-6.

[3] Grahame Clark, 'The Economic Approach to Prehistory', *Proceedings of the British Academy*, 39 (1953), 215-38.

[4] Cf. the words drafted by the present writer for *Archaeology and Government* (Rescue and the Council for British Archaeology, London, 1974), para. 2.2, which were composed in the light of this Winchester experience, and the surprised reaction to them of F. H. Thompson, 'Rescue Archaeology: Research or Rubbish Collection?', *Antiquity*, 49 (1975), 43-5.

From the very start our intention was not only to look at the changing chances of the city through time, but also to explore contemporary variations between one part of the city and another in successive phases of Winchester's development. At a rather superficial level this study of what some would now call intra-site variation was required as a foil to the study of the great buildings of church and state with which the project was concerned *ab initio*. Only thus could one really appreciate the role such structures played in contemporary society, the relative effort their construction and maintenance involved, and the quality of the achievement they represented.[1] At a more profound level, the study of the urban phenomenon required for the characterization of its successive phases a broadly based exploration of the fabric of the city, across the full range of variation in wealth, class, and occupation. This involved more than gross distinctions between castle, palace, and monastery on the one hand and the 'ordinary' inhabited areas of the city on the other. At an early stage in the Lower Brook Street excavation the problem was defined as distinguishing the typical and the exceptional, among the medieval houses on that site,[2] but it soon developed into a more sophisticated study of variation, both in the archaeology of the Lower Brook Street sites and in the study of the documentary evidence for the city as a whole from the eleventh century onwards.[3]

With many of these requirements in mind a scheme for the development of the Winchester project over a total term of ten years (1961–70) was sketched out in the back of the director's field notebook during the summer of 1964.[4] In the event an extra season was needed in 1971 to complete the necessary objectives, and even so some of the ideas of 1964 had been too ambitious to be practicable.[5] During those years the Iron Age enclosure was

[1] For a contrary view, provoked by the emergence of a truly 'new' medieval archaeology, see Joan Evans, 'Anniversary Address', *Antiquaries Journal*, 41 (1961), 152.

[2] III. Interim, p. 246.

[3] Winchester Studies 1 (*Winchester in the Early Middle Ages*) deals with the period from the late ninth to the late twelfth century on the basis of an edition and discussion of the Winton Domesday. Winchester Studies 2 (*Survey of Medieval Winchester*) by Dr Derek Keene covers essentially the period between the thirteenth and the sixteenth centuries and by tracing the tenure of virtually every tenement in the walled city and its ancient suburbs establishes the base for, and undertakes a comprehensive discussion of, the economic and social geography of medieval Winchester.

[4] Winchester Research Unit, SNB, vol. 61, p. 74.

[5] It envisaged, for example, the complete excavation of New Minster and much more work in Lower Brook Street than actually proved possible.

defined and dated. The Roman defences were investigated in detail at five points, and areas of the Roman town were thoroughly examined for the first time, including several streets, parts of the forum, a temple, five town houses, and a number of other buildings. The Anglo-Saxon cathedral, the Old Minster, was fully excavated except for the part lying below the present cathedral (Pls. 11, 12a). The New Minster was identified and its later domestic buildings explored. The royal castle was excavated at its northern end (Pl. 13); the bishop's palace completely explored (Pl. 14); in addition, two parish churches (Pl. 15a), three chapels (Pl. 13b), and twelve medieval houses (Pl. 15b) were uncovered. Most important, perhaps, was the demonstration that the street plan of medieval and modern Winchester derived from a deliberate act of urban refoundation in the later ninth century (Fig. 4).[1] All told, nineteen sites were investigated over eleven years at a total cost of £149,811, with the help of about 3,000 volunteers (no one was paid anything other than daily subsistence), from twenty-four countries.[2] Most of the work took place within the walls, where 11,612 m² (1.16 ha) were excavated to an average depth of 2.5 m. Outside the walls an additional 2,631 m² were investigated, usually to a much shallower depth. The cost of excavation (excluding Lankhills) worked out at £12·17 per m².

By 1966 it was already clear that the great mass of data resulting from the six seasons of excavation so far undertaken, together with that from the four seasons planned for 1967–70, could not be properly analysed and published on a part-time basis by volunteers. A visit to Poland at the invitation of Professor Witold Hensel of the Institute for the History of Material Culture of the Polish Academy of Sciences in September 1966, to see the work being carried on in Polish towns—especially, Wrocław, Poznań,

[1] II. Interim, pp. 215–17; III. Interim, p. 242; VIII. Interim, pp. 285–9; X. Interim, pp. 101–4; Martin Biddle and David Hill, 'Late Saxon Planned Towns', *Antiquaries Journal*, 51 (1971), 70–85; Winchester Studies, 1, pp. 277–82; and see below, pp. 325–32.

[2] For details of the development of the project and its administration, see I–X. Interims; Biddle, 'Winchester 1961–68', *Château Gaillard* iv (1969), 19–30; and idem, *Archaeology in Winchester* (typescript prepared for the new Winchester City District Council following local government reorganization, Apr. 1974). From 1964 to 1970 the University of North Carolina and Duke University in the United States played a vital role in the provision of both student volunteers and funds (£27,761 or 18.5 per cent of the total cost of the excavations), a collaboration pioneered by the late Professor Urban T. Holmes of the University of North Carolina.

Gdańsk, and Szczecin[1]—suggested that the best solution would be the creation for a period of years of a full-time team to undertake the work of preparing the results of the Winchester excavations and associated research for publication. As a result the Winchester Research Unit was set up in October 1968 to produce a series of eleven volumes of Winchester Studies for publication by the Clarendon Press at Oxford.[2] Three volumes have now been published, a fourth is in proof, and others are far advanced, several of them in their final stages of completion. The range of volumes reflects to the full the scope of the Winchester project. In addition to formal excavation reports, there are two volumes on the tenurial, economic, and social history of the medieval city, set firmly in a physical setting derived from documentary, topographical, and archaeological sources. Another volume deals with the production of the Winchester mint, an essential source for the economic and social history of the city between the late ninth century and the middle of the thirteenth, and is of special numismatic importance as only the second such study of a major mint. Other volumes deal with the medieval pottery of Winchester; with its crafts and industries; with its human and animal populations; and with the evidence for the environment of the city from the Roman period to the Middle Ages.

By the time the Winchester Research Unit began work in 1968, there had already been eight seasons of excavation and three more were to come. There was therefore never any real question of publishing in fascicules, although this was already established practice for urban excavations in the classical world, such as the Agora at Athens or Dura-Europos. Instead, we decided to publish the series of substantial, digested, thematic volumes which are now appearing. There is no doubt that this has taken a long time, and that the publication of a series of fascicules might have looked better, but I am reasonably sure that the late start of the Research Unit relative to the excavations themselves will in the end be seen as a blessing in disguise. Because each of the volumes is able to draw on the results of the whole excavation and all the associated research, it can be not only complete in itself, but can be selective

---

[1] For the Polish achievement, see, for example, Pierre Francastel (ed.), *Les origines des villes polonaises* (Paris, 1960); Witold Hensel, *Słowiańszczyzna wczesnośredniowieczna* (Warsaw, 1965), translated as *Die Slawen im frühen Mittelalter* (Berlin, 1965); idem, *La naissance de la Pologne* (Warsaw, 1966); and the fascicules of *Archaeologia Urbium* published under the auspices of the Union internationale des sciences préhistoriques et protohistoriques (Warsaw), Fasc. 1 (1966) et seqq. [2] For a list, see Appendix B.

in a way in which a fascicule series published as the work goes
along can never be. Moreover, the Winchester volumes, although
admittedly expensive in themselves, are actually turning out
somewhat cheaper, page for page, than fascicules. If one adds the
saving which comes from avoiding unnecessary duplication in
publication, a problem which unavoidably affects fascicules, the
cost-effectiveness of the substantive volume may be considerable.

The need to be selective in publication, on grounds of both cost
and clarity, became clear very early in the Winchester project.
The methods of open-area excavation, developed initially as early
as 1964-5 to deal with the complexities of medieval house sites
continuously occupied for over five centuries in Lower Brook
Street,[1] demanded plans as subtle and detailed as the sections,
which had long been (and still continue to be) a fundamental
element in British archaeological practice. The need to compare
the plans of successive surfaces led to the introduction of
dimensionally stable transparent drawing film which allowed us
to lay one plan over another. A proper record of what our
excavations were themselves destroying required the production
of plans of a long sequence of successive surfaces. For example, the
church of St Mary in Tanner Street required twenty-six plans
properly to record the horizontal evidence of its long structural
history, a sequence which provided the first-recorded pattern of
change in the liturgical planning of an urban church over a period
of more than half a millenium.[2] The detail to be recorded, much
of it fundamental, also required the use, indeed the introduction, of colour on the drawings. These two factors—the quantity of
the records and the use of colour—implied from the start that the
days of publishing everything, if indeed they ever existed, were
over, and in Winchester we never contemplated doing this.

The complexity of the records arose inevitably from an increasing awareness of the complexity of urban sites and the need to
record this complexity as fully as possible if it was to be understood
at all. An outline record, in my view, was worse than useless
because it was itself a falsification, an oversimplification to the
point where the result might be in very fact more misleading than
informative. As an example of the kind of detail encountered—
none of it to be dismissed as 'trivial'—let us take one trench of

[1] III. Interim, p. 245; IV. Interim, p. 313; Martin Biddle and Birthe
Kjølbye-Biddle, 'Metres, Areas and Robbing', *World Archaeology*, 1 (1969-70),
208-19.
[2] VII. Interim, pp. 305-9, fig. 2; X Interim, pp. 312-14, fig. 15. The final
publication will be in Winchester Studies 5.

63 m² in the excavation of Old Minster (CG 1966–8, Trench XXXIII; Pl. 12a): it included four robber-trenches, fourteen walls, twenty-nine pits, seven post-holes, 122 graves, and 893 layers. These required for their recording (and the list is not quite complete), 480 pages of notes in six notebooks; fifty-eight coloured plans of 961 m² of deposit at a scale of 1:20; seventy-nine coloured drawings of 209 m of section at a scale of 1:10; 172 photographs (149 in both black and white and colour); and some 5,000 level measurements. The excavation of this trench lasted for thirty-two weeks spread over three seasons, but it was only one of fifty-one trenches on the Cathedral Green between 1962 and 1970. The publication of such a complex in a single volume of Winchester Studies (Volume 4. i) requires the most careful selection and presentation of the evidence if a true and reliable picture is to be given. It also implies the need for adequate time fully to analyse such an archive in the course of preparing the final publication— and this is what the Winchester Research Unit is all about—as well as provision for the long-term public storage of all the detailed evidence upon which the distillation in the published volume is based. Why should we bother to store the evidence, once the final publication is out? Precisely because the record was made in the first place to be reinterrogated at any time in the future, in the light of new knowledge, new ideas, new parallels. Did we make the right deductions from what we thought we saw and recorded? Did we understand what we were recording? The published volumes of Winchester Studies will state our views. The recorded evidence—subjective as it may be—should be available as a primary source for as long as necessary, perhaps for ever, ready to support or disprove alternative interpretations.

This too was fully in mind when the Research Unit was set up in 1968. The indexing of the archive was one of our first concerns, partly to help ourselves, partly because the published volumes will carry references to the excavation archive, comparable to the references to documentary sources in our historical studies, which will enable the reader, however far away he or she may be, to call for copies of the original records to satisfy doubts or to form the base of a new view. The use of colour in the plans and sections caused us some initial concern, but consultation with representatives of IBM and Xerox in 1968 revealed that colour-xerography was on the way, and indeed it was with us ten years later.

Finding a home for the excavation archive—defined as the total information product: records, finds, samples, analyses, reports, computer discs and tapes—was for long a major problem, but after some years of uncertainty the Winchester City Council decided to go ahead with the conversion of Hyde House and Hyde Barn, outside North Gate, into an Historic Resources Centre.[1] This Centre, which is an integral part of the Winchester City Museums under the curator Miss E. R. Lewis, FMA, now houses the total information product of the work of 1961 to 1971 and of the Winchester Research Unit, as well as the results of previous and subsequent excavations in Winchester. It was opened in 1981 and is the first purpose-built archive of the kind in the country. It is the essential companion to the publication of our work in Winchester Studies.

The completion of the Winchester Excavation Committee's eleven-year programme of excavations in 1971 did not mean that the archaeology of Winchester was in any sense done and could now be left to gradual erosion by further development. Quite the reverse: with the knowledge gained from the work of 1961–71 it was now possible to define much more clearly the questions that should be asked. Moreover, the pace of development, far from slackening, was about to increase and an inner ring road seemed at last about to be built.

Although the City Museums had continued throughout the sixties to be responsible for the observation and recording of archaeological discoveries made during building works in the city, all excavations had been undertaken by the Committee. Now some new arrangement was necessary if rescue excavations were to take place in the future. Late in 1971 the City Council accepted the recommendation that a City Rescue Archaeologist should be appointed to take charge of all rescue archaeology in the city, including both the observation and recording of sites in the course of development and the conduct of excavations on threatened sites prior to the start of works. The first holder of the post was appointed early in 1972 and later the same year the current holder, Mr Kenneth Qualmann, was appointed in his stead. Following the reorganization of local government in 1974 the responsibilities of the office were extended to the whole of the new District. Until 1977 the Rescue Archaeologist and his staff were seconded to the Research Unit, which was responsible for the overall conduct and policy of his work, but in 1977, when a start

[1] See the printed proposal *Historic Resources Centre for Winchester* (Winchester City Council, 1976); *Rescue News*, 24 (Dec. 1980), 4; *Architectural Journal*, 14 Oct. 1981, pp. 736–7; Elizabeth Lewis, 'Winchester City Museums', in *Archaeological Storage* (Society of Museum Archaeologists and Yorkshire and Humberside Federation of Museums and Art Galleries, 1981), p. 34.

was made on running down the Research Unit, rescue archaeology reverted to the care of the City Museums where it remains.

In the eleven years since the office was established, rescue archaeology in Winchester has been very much a full-time activity.[1] Partly as a result of deliberate policy, partly because of the geographical concentration of major developments outside the walls, the work has been the perfect complement to that of 1961–71 (Fig. 1). Whereas the Excavation Committee (WEC) conducted fourth-fifths of its work inside the walls, the City Rescue Archaeologist (CRA) has done nine-tenths of his work in the suburbs:

	Years	Inside the walls	In the suburbs	Totals
WEC	1961–71	11,612 m²	2,631 m²	14,243 m²
CRA	1972–83	577 m²	5,263 m²	5,840 m²
Totals		12,189 m²	7,894 m²	20,083 m²

Knowledge of the Iron Age 'Oram's Arbour' enclosure has been considerably extended, particularly with regard to its entrances and subsequent influence on early Roman Winchester (Fig. 3). The Cirencester road has been studied in detail as it approaches North Gate, together with suburban developments along the road and cemeteries of the first to second and fourth to fifth centuries AD. Further information about the eastern and western cemeteries has also been recovered. The early medieval development of the northern and especially the western suburbs has been examined, and within the walls work has been carried out on the castle, on St Mary's Abbey (Nunnaminster), and as a preliminary to large-scale redevelopment of the central car park. The results are being prepared for publication in a series of volumes edited by Mr Kenneth Qualmann under the title *Winchester Excavations since 1972*.[2]

It is vital to stress the value of this work. Far from being an example of diminishing returns, the discoveries of 1972 onwards

[1] Kenneth Qualmann, 'Rescue Archaeology in the City of Winchester', *District Councils Review*, Mar. 1975; and the successive numbers of *Find* (Newsletter of the Winchester Archaeological Rescue Group), 1 (Oct. 1972)–43 (Sept. 1987), continued as *Winchester Museums Service Newsletter*, 1 (June, 1988) onwards.

[2] Vol. 1 will deal with excavations in the western suburbs; Vol. 2 with Wickham Glebe, a site in the District outside the former boundaries of the city; Vol. 3 with excavations in the northern suburbs. In some cases, where convenience or other circumstances dictate, reports or other results of the work of the City Rescue Archaeologist will be found in *Winchester Excavations*

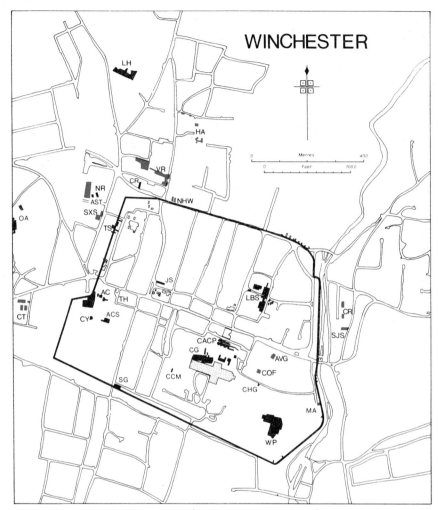

Fig. 1. Excavations in Winchester 1961–83: the continued investment. Sites excavated 1961–71 by the Winchester Excavations Committee (including Lankhills, excavated 1967–72 by the Winchester Schools Archaeological Committee) are shown in black; those excavated 1972–83 by the City Rescue Archaeologist are shown in blue.

have emphasized the importance of building on investment and of continuing work in a place where sufficient has been done to allow questions to be framed with precision and reframed to the degree

1949–1960 (see above, p. 300 n. 4), e.g. 'St. Paul's Church' in ibid. 2 (1978), 264–79 and cf. p. 1; or in Winchester Studies, e.g., the gazetteer of prehistoric and Roman sites in Winchester Studies, 3. i, or the account of the first excavation of part of the Nunnaminster (St Mary's Abbey) in Winchester Studies 4. i. For an especially important discovery, see also David A. Hinton, Suzanne Keene, and Kenneth E. Qualmann, 'The Winchester Reliquary', *Medieval Archaeology* 25 (1981), 45–77.

where reasonably sophisticated answers can be obtained. The
City Council and the Department of the Environment are to be
congratulated for taking this view and for not accepting the
simplistic argument, heard all too often in the stress of funding
crisis, that 'it's all been done' or 'there can't be any more to do'.
The extent to which the investment of over thirty years of archaeological and historical research into Winchester now allows us to
formulate questions for future inquiry is the subject of the next
sections of this lecture. Questions such as these will only be
answered by the continued activity of the City Rescue Archaeologist and his voluntary support-group WARG (the Winchester
Archaeological Rescue Group) in the context of the city as a
designated area of archaeological importance under the 1979
Act.[1] The City Council is now proposing to designate the whole of
the ancient walled city and suburbs as such an area and is one of
the first local authorities attempting to do so under the Act.[2]

II

The excavations of 1961–71 investigated just under 2 per cent of
the walled area, a figure which the work of 1972–83 has barely
affected. One must ask whether any generalizing statements
about the city's past can be justified on so limited a base. The
answer is that the sites comprising the 2 per cent were themselves
carefully selected with both general and specific problems in mind
and that, justified or not, such statements must be made, if only as
the starting-points for the next stage of enquiry. But the smallness
of the evidential foundation must be kept in mind at all times: it
is indeed the reason for some of the more radical questions and
ideas I intend to propose. The existence of an increasing body of
documentary evidence from the eleventh century onwards provides, of course, a wider context in which ideas derived from the
inevitably much more limited archaeological base can be tested,
but one must remember that the kinds of interpretation derived
from the archaeological evidence may not be testable through the
documents and vice versa. For the first thousand years of
Winchester's existence, however, the problem scarcely arises, for
although almost the entire development of the city belongs to the
period of literacy in Britain, its history as a town before the tenth,
perhaps even the eleventh century, is unwritten. We are dealing

[1] Ancient Monuments and Archaeological Areas Act 1979.
[2] Qualmann, 'Designation of an "Archaeological Area" at Winchester',
Find, 32 (Jan. 1984), 11–14.

throughout this early period as regards most aspects of Winchester —certainly its urban aspects—if not with a prehistoric, then at most with a protohistoric community.

Let us look first at the only general interpretation of the origin and development of Winchester published so far (Fig. 2). It appeared in 1965, and was revised in 1968 and again in 1975.[1] This model stressed topographical change, especially increase and contraction in the occupied area. It made the point that in the course of many centuries an urban community could wax and wane, changing, perhaps more than once, from urban to non-urban status and back again. This aspect seemed especially important because discussion of the 'continuity question' was often hampered then—it is even now—by an imprecision of terms. Continuity of urban life is something quite different from continuity of life in former urban places. Until this was clear, the discussion could not (and did not) proceed.

The gross changes revealed in these diagrams have now been plotted for a number of other towns, large and small.[2] The exercise has been useful. It provides several bases for comparison between towns and it brings out many points of both general and detailed change—the establishment of a street plan, the growth of a suburb, the presence or absence of major topographical, social, and economic units, such as a castle or a religious house—but useful as they may be in making comparisons and in calling attention to relationships in time and space, such diagrams are only a very simple tool. What they reflect, like topographical change itself, are profound alterations of function in urban places. The definition of such functional change should be a fundamental goal of urban archaeology and of urban history in general, and it is in the framework of functional change that I want briefly to review our current knowledge of the development of early Winchester.

A good case can be made out for describing the site of Winchester as a preferred location for settlement. This presumably reflects the natural advantages of valley and downland which were exploited from at least the second millennium BC for travel on routes which crossed at the site of Winchester.[3] The Iron Age

[1] *Science Journal*, Mar. 1965, pp. 4–5; VI. Interim, fig. 1; X. Interim, fig. 21.

[2] For example, London, Biddle and Hudson, op. cit. above, p. 300 n. 3, fig. 9; and Saffron Walden, S. R. Bassett, *Saffron Walden: Excavations and Research 1972–80* (Council for British Archaeology, Research Report 45, London, 1982), fig. 4.

[3] Initial discussion in C. F. C. Hawkes, J. N. L. Myres, and C. G. Stevens, *St. Catharine's Hill, Winchester* (Winchester, 1930), pp. 5–6, fig. 3; for Middle and Late Bronze Age sites at and in the immediate vicinity of Winchester, see Sonia Chadwick Hawkes, 'Finds from Two Middle Bronze Age Pits at

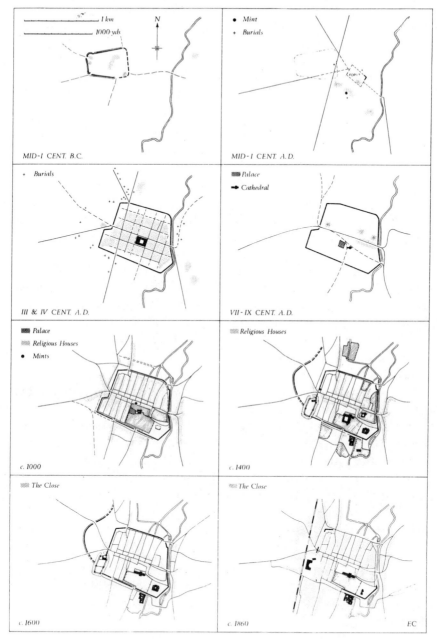

FIG. 2. The development of Winchester. Occupied areas stippled in blue. (Revised to 1983.)

Winnall, Winchester, Hampshire', *Proceedings of the Hampshire Field Club*, 26 (1969), 5–18, esp. fig. 1; Collis, *Winchester Excavations 1949–60*, 2 (1978), 109, 121, 161, 200 (*pace* Collis, p. 4, the evidence clearly shows that Bronze Age activity was *relatively* intense in the area); and, for the latest (1982) discoveries at Easton Lane, Richard Whinney in *Find*, 29 (Jan. 1983), 5–10.

hillfort on St Catharine's Hill, preceded from perhaps the fifth
century BC by an unenclosed settlement on that dominating and
isolated down, reflects the growing centrality of the Winchester
area in the third century.[1]

On the opposite side of the valley, on the site of the later walled
city, a local concentration of settlement is characterized by the
same kind of pottery (the 'St Catharine's Hill Group') as is found
in the later phases on St Catharine's Hill.[2] Enclosed settlement on
the Hill and unenclosed settlement at Winchester are probably in
part contemporary, but at Winchester the pottery tradition seems
to develop further than on the Hill, where the entrance to the
hillfort was burnt and the site abandoned perhaps about 100 BC.

During the currency of pottery types of the St Catharine's Hill
Group an area of 16 ha (41 acres) on the Winchester site was
enclosed by a line of bank and ditch (Fig. 3). The enclosure lies on
the hill slope, partly below the north-west corner of the Roman
town, but mostly without and to the west of the walled area.
Entrances have been excavated at Oram's Arbour on the west and
tentatively identified at the point where Romsey Road now
crosses the ditch to the south-west, at Trafalgar House to the
south, and at the site of the later North Gate.[3]

Three major questions remain unsettled: the status of this
enclosed settlement; the period during which it was in use; and its
relationship to the Roman town.

Collis considers that the Oram's Arbour enclosed settlement did
not cross 'the threshold of urbanisation',[4] but there is much to
support the opposite view. The scale of the public works involved
in making the bank and ditch (1.7 km, 1.06 miles, in length); the
area enclosed (16.5 ha, 84 per cent larger than the area enclosed
on St Catharine's Hill); the multiple entrances with their evident
relationship to the long-distance routes of the area; the presence of
imported amphorae of Dressel Type I (from the lower, but not the
lowest, fill of the ditch);[5] and the remarkable concentration of
native and imported coins, Ptolemaic, Massiliot, and Gaulish;[6] all

---

[1] Christopher Hawkes, 'St. Catharine's Hill, Winchester: the Report of 1930
Re-assessed', in D. W. Harding (ed.), *Hillforts* (London, New York, San
Francisco, 1976), pp. 59–74.

[2] Cunliffe, *Winchester Excavations 1949–60*, 1 (1964), 1–6; Collis, *Winchester
Excavations 1949–60*, 2 (1978), 3–6.   [3] X. Interim, pp. 98–100, fig. 1.

[4] *Winchester Excavations 1949–60*, 2 (1978), 6.

[5] X. Interim, pp. 99–100.

[6] Biddle, 'Ptolemaic Coins from Winchester, *Antiquity*, 49 (1975), 213–15,
fig. 1, based on the work of the late Mr Derek Allen to be published in
Winchester Studies 3. i.

these make a case for a pre-Roman oppidum at Winchester albeit not in the immediate pre-Roman period.

The chronological problems are indeed formidable: not only the fine chronology involved in deciding which components of this settlement belong together (for example, which of the coins derives instead from the earliest Roman activity on the site),[1] but also the chronology of the enclosed settlement itself. The defences were certainly constructed after, perhaps long after, the first appearance of pottery of the St Catharine's Hill Group on the site; they were probably constructed after, perhaps well after, the abandonment of St Catharine's Hill itself. But how long do they continue to define an associated settlement? Pottery of what might be a later, even an immediately pre-Roman, phase occurs in the latest pre-Roman filling of the Iron Age ditch on the Assize Courts site. Its significance is quite unclear. Does it represent continued use of the enclosure, or its disuse and the shift of settlement south and east into areas of Winchester which have never been archaeologically examined (cf. Fig. 1)? How long, if at all, was the site deserted before the Roman arrival? And to what extent do we mean 'desertion' as an absolute or a relative description?

The problem is of particular importance in relation to the role played by the Oram's Arbour earthwork in the emergence of Roman Winchester. It has been clear for some time that the presence of the Iron Age earthworks had a considerable topographical effect—but that could be due simply to their bulk, to their role as relict features and 'morphological frames' long after they had gone out of use. As work goes on, however, the closeness of the mesh between the earthworks and the earliest Roman roads becomes ever more striking (Fig. 3): it now looks as if the Cirencester and Silchester roads are making for an Iron Age entrance on the site of North Gate, and the Old Sarum road for an entrance at the south-west corner of the Iron Age enclosure. The entrance excavated at Oram's Arbour in 1967 was likewise occupied by a Roman road, albeit a late and minor one.

The significance of these observations will only become clear with further work on the Iron Age earthworks themselves, on the settlement they enclose, and on the early Roman long-distance

---

[1] On this problem, and for the differing views of Collis and Cunliffe on the status of pre-Roman Winchester, see Cunliffe (ed.), *Coinage and Society in Britain and Gaul: Some Current Problems* (Council for British Archaeology, Research Report 38, 1981), p. 54, cf. fig. 15, and see the review by P. H. Robinson, *British Numismatic Journal*, 51 (1981), 204-5.

roads. Enough has been said, however, to indicate how twenty years of intermittent observation and excavation have only served to stress and to define, but not to solve the problems of Iron Age Winchester and of the beginnings of urbanization in the Itchen valley.

This short consideration of pre-Roman Winchester has already served to define a brief florescence—whether urban or not—which probably died away before the Roman arrival. It has also shown how very incomplete our evidence is. When we turn to the origins and subsequent fortunes of the walled city of 58.2 ha (143.8 acres), we must always remember that only 1.22 ha (3.01 acres) has been excavated within the walls in the last twenty-two years (1961–83): a mere 2.1 per cent. Obviously something can be added to this for the excavations of 1949–60, and to allow for the sites which have been observed in the course of building work, but in both these categories the quality of the evidence is less than satisfactory. This very small percentage—2.1 per cent—means not only that we must be cautious in putting forward general views (or at least cautious in how much weight we put upon them), but also that we must be very careful indeed in arguing from negative evidence. In urban archaeology as a whole, not least in Winchester, negative evidence is at best a dangerous and often, perhaps usually, a misleading guide.

Roman Winchester (*Venta Belgarum*) was the fifth largest city of Roman Britain in terms of walled area and, as its name implies, the principal town of the *civitas* of the Belgae. Like many of the other towns of Roman Britain, the Roman origins of *Venta* may be with the establishment of a military fort,[1] intended here, as elsewhere, to control important routes and a centre of British settlement (dispersed settlement, perhaps, if the Oram's Arbour enclosure was by then abandoned). The earliest phases of Roman Winchester are extremely difficult to reach: over nearly half the walled area they are waterlogged and everywhere they are covered by deep medieval deposits of the greatest complexity and interest. There are hints, however, that the earliest stages of Roman Winchester are anything but simple: the course and early date of the Silchester–Bitterne road;[2] its route to the west of the supposed

---

[1] X. Interim, pp. 296–7, figs. 10, 11, and 21. No further discoveries relating to the possible fort have been made since 1971.

[2] At South Gate (X. Interim, p. 110) this road precedes the early Flavian timber gate and runs north to North Gate on a line which appears unrelated to the possible fort in the flood-plain to the east (cf. here fig. 2, mid first century AD).

fort and its relationship to the Iron Age earthwork (Fig. 2); the early and unexplained salient at the south-west angle of the later first-century defences; and the gradual realization that there is a street layout in and outside the north-west corner of the walled area on a different alignment to the rest of the street grid[1]—all these suggest that our knowledge of early *Venta* is a sketch, and possibly a misleading one at that.

We are perhaps on slightly safer ground from the Flavian period onwards. Whatever went before, the evidence from all over the town suggests a massive intensification of activity. Defences of earth and timber were thrown up to south, west, and north on the line that was to be followed by all subsequent walls; the main street grid was laid out; and thoroughly Romanized timber buildings with tiled roofs, painted walls, glazed windows, and the occasional mosaic floor were constructed. This marks the first phase of full urbanization. Whether the previous Roman phases were urban, or simply the surviving *vici* of an earlier military occupation, we do not yet know, but there is no doubt that the establishment of full urban status was sudden and that it took place in the seventies of the first century AD. The immediate reasons for this change may be in part political or dynastic, as has been suggested,[2] but the change would have been stillborn had it not responded to underlying processes which fostered the existence of an economic, social, and administrative centre at *Venta*.

III

It is not possible to trace here the development of *Venta* in the second, third, and earlier fourth centuries.[3] In the sequence of its defences, public buildings and town houses, it seems, so far as we can see, to have followed a pattern common to the Roman towns of south-central Britain. Shortly after AD 350 the character of the town changed, perhaps quite suddenly. All seven of the town houses of which sufficient is known went out of use at this time.[4] In most cases they were demolished and their sites cleared and

[1] I am grateful to Mr K. Qualmann for this information.

[2] Anthony A. Barrett, 'The Career of Tiberius Claudius Cogidubnus', *Britannia*, 10 (1979), 227–42, esp. 240; cf. J. E. Bogaers, 'King Cogidubnus in Chichester: Another Reading of *RIB* 91', ibid., pp. 243–54, esp. pp. 252–4.

[3] *Winchester Studies*, 3. i will include a full discussion, together with a gazetteer of all previous discoveries relating to prehistoric and Roman Winchester.

[4] Cathedral Car Park, Building 1 (S.E.): I. Interim, pp. 155–6 (demolition redated to *c*.350); Wolvesey Palace, Buildings West 1, East 1A, 1B, 2, 3: X. Interim, pp. 321–4, fig. 17; and houses in Middle Brook Street and St George's Street.

fenced. In some cases industrial activity, or a kind of domestic use very different from what had gone before, took over. In one case a small, rectangular, two-roomed structure was built alongside a street over part of a demolished house. This two-roomed building cannot have been built before the second half of the fourth century; in its date and situation it recalls a comparable structure found by Professor Frere in Dorchester on Thames in 1962.[1] At the same time occupation, as reflected in the distribution of pottery and coins, seems to have spread for the first time over the whole walled area of Winchester, the western third of which, at least, had until then been only lightly used. This extended occupation is characterized by the 'dark earth' layer which is found all over the walled area on top of the Roman deposits,[2] and also by the presence for the first time in the Roman period of relatively large quantities of iron-working residues.[3]

The disuse of houses and the presence of the 'dark earth' have usually been taken as evidence of 'decline' or 'decay'. It is doubtful, however, if this view can be maintained. The town's defences were strengthened in the second half of the fourth century by the addition of bastions, one of which has been partly excavated at South Gate and a second tentatively identified to the south of West Gate.[4] Outside the walls, although the suburbs may be smaller, there appears to be a remarkable increase in the size of the cemeteries.[5] Kenneth Qualmann has estimated that, of the

[1] X. Interim, pp. 324–6; cf. Sheppard Frere, 'Excavations at Dorchester on Thames, 1962', *Archaeological Journal*, 119 (1962), 120–3, figs. 5 and 6, and idem, 'The End of Towns in Roman Britain', in J. S. Wacher (ed.), *The Civitas Capitals of Roman Britain* (Leicester, 1966), p. 94. For a rural building of the same type and date, see D. S. Neal, *The Excavation of the Roman Villa in Gadebridge Park, Hemel Hempstead, 1963–8* (Society of Antiquaries, Research Report 31, London 1974), pp. 57–8, fig. 32, pl. xixa (Building E).

[2] R. I. Macphail, 'Soil and Botanical Studies of the Dark Earth', in M. Jones and G. W. Dimbleby (eds.), *The Environment of Man* (British Archaeological Reports, British Series 87, Oxford 1981), pp. 309–31; and idem., 'The Micromorphology of Dark Earth from Gloucester, London and Norwich: an Analysis of Urban Anthropogenic Deposits from the Late Roman to Early Medieval Periods in England', in P. Bullock and C. Murphy (eds.), *Soil Micromorphology*, i (Proceedings of the International Working-Meeting on Soil Micromorphology, Aug. 1981, Oxford, 1983), 245–52.

[3] Identified by R. F. Tylecote and quantified by R. Davies and D. L. Long for publication in Winchester Studies, 3. i and 7. ii.

[4] For the bastion at South Gate, see X. Interim, pp. 115–16; the possible bastion south of West Gate is reported (pers. comm.) by Mr K. Qualmann as a result of his excavations against the outside of the Roman city wall at the south end of Castle Avenue.   [5] See Winchester Studies, 3. ii, pp. 5–7, figs. 1 and 2.

approximately 1,300 graves so far recorded, over a thousand belong to the third and fourth centuries, and most of these to the fourth century. Nor is there any indication of any marked decrease in burial in the second half of the fourth century.[1]

All this suggests that *Venta* underwent a considerable change in the later fourth century, but not that it was necessarily in decline or decay.[2] To the contrary, one could argue from the size and density of the occupied area, from the evidence of industrial activity and from the cemeteries, that late Roman Winchester was more urban than it had ever been. The closest parallel might be a densely occupied, industrially and commercially active, pre-Roman oppidum,[3] or its post-Roman analogue, a maritime trading and industrial settlement such as Anglo-Saxon Southampton.[4]

Late Roman *Venta* was clearly different from what had gone before. The city was not kept clean and the roads were no longer swept and regravelled, but it was occupied and it was defended. What sort of place was it? A useful analogy may perhaps be provided in reverse by the changes which took place in late medieval and early modern Winchester.[5] The textile industry and commercial functions of medieval Winchester finally collapsed in the sixteenth and early seventeenth centuries to be replaced in the later seventeenth century by the rise of the city as a centre for county society, characterized by large town houses and an expanding retail market serving both the specialized needs of the gentry and the increased purchasing power of those dependent on them. The administrative role of the city as an ecclesiastical and legal centre continued throughout, but it is interesting to observe

---

[1] For example, at Lankhills in the northern cemetery, Winchester Studies, 3. ii, pp. 113-22; or at Chester Road in the eastern, *Find*, 21 (May 1980), 3-4, and phased plans. At Victoria Road, outside North Gate, a new cemetery came into use *c*.350, *Find*, 11 (winter 1975), 5-7.

[2] Cf. Susan Reynolds, 'Decline and Decay in Late Medieval Towns: a Look at some of the Concepts and Arguments', *Urban History Yearbook 1980*, pp. 76-8. For another view of late Romano-British towns, see Richard Reece, 'Town and Country: the end of Roman Britain', *World Archaeology*, 12 (1980), 77-92.

[3] See Barry Cunliffe and Trevor Rowley, *Oppida in Barbarian Europe* (British Archaeological Reports, Supplementary Series 11, Oxford, 1976).

[4] See now Philip Holdsworth, *Excavations at Melbourne Street, Southampton, 1971-76* (Southampton Archaeological Research Committee, Report 1; Council for British Archaeology, Research Report 33, London, 1980) with full bibliography; see also idem, 'Saxon Southampton; a New Review', *Medieval Archaeology*, 20 (1976), 26-61.

[5] Adrienne Rosen, 'Winchester in Transition, 1580-1700', in Peter Clark (ed.), *Country Towns in Pre-industrial England* (Leicester, 1981), pp. 143-95.

that when that administrative role also faltered, for example in the 1540s after the Dissolution and in the 1640s during the Civil War, Winchester's fortunes reached their lowest ebb.

The analogy between Roman *Venta* of the late first to mid fourth centuries and later seventeenth-century Winchester is clear: both were administrative centres with a special attraction for the gentry and retail markets to suit their needs. The difference may be that, whereas in the sixteenth century Winchester was abandoning its industrial function, in the later fourth century *Venta* changed rather rapidly, perhaps very suddenly, in the reverse direction, facilities for the gentry, such as town houses, being removed in favour of something very different.

The very small area examined within the walls must counsel caution: change in one area, even in several areas of the walled town, might not apply to other areas, but the functional change suggested here as a model for the later fourth century can be tested as further sites become available.

Was Winchester in the later fourth century urban, or was it simply a military or industrial centre, or all three? They are, after all, not necessarily exclusive functions. We cannot yet answer this question, but the place-name may provide a clue.[1] In common with most other Romano-British *civitas* capitals, the tribal element in the name *Venta Belgarum* was lost. Subsequently *Venta* acquired the Old English suffix *ceaster*. The usual view would see the element *ceaster* as a generalized Old English description for a Roman walled town or ruin, derived from Latin *castrum*, but without specific military meaning.[2] The stages by which *Venta Belgarum* became *Wintanceaster* seem, however, to merit further and comparative study, to establish whether the sequence might have included the usage *Castrum Venta* or *Venta castrum* in the military sense. Late Roman *Venta* with its refurbished defences, plentiful population, industrial activity, and internal compounds, might after all have had an important military function, if not as a fortress, then as a defended administrative base and supply centre dealing with the *annona militaris*.[3] The *gynaeceum* at *Venta* mentioned

[1] For the importance of place-names in general for the study of early Winchester, see Winchester Studies, 1, pp. 231-9.

[2] See the valuable discussion, stressing the need for further work on this place-name element, by Margaret Gelling, *Signposts to the Past* (London, 1979), pp. 151-3.

[3] For the *annona* itself, see Walter Goffart, *Caput and Colonate: towards a History of Late Roman Taxation* (Toronto, 1974), pp. 31-54; and for the suggestion that the defended towns were important for the protection of the *annona*, see Derek A. Welsby, *The Roman Military Defence of the British Provinces in its Later*

in the *Notitia Dignitatum* would be entirely at home in such a base and might even be its *raison d'être*.[1] The production of textiles in a *gynaeceum* would leave archaeological traces, but conditions for the recovery and correct interpretation of the fulling and dyeing vats, the weaving and drying sheds, would be difficult to fulfil in a town where the later Roman levels have been so damaged by subsequent activity.[2] The search for such traces remains nevertheless a high priority. The possibility of a textile industry of this date stresses the aptness of the analogy drawn earlier between late Roman and later medieval Winchester. The closing down of a *gynaeceum* in 407 might also account for the sudden collapse of later Roman Winchester seen so vividly in the abandonment of organized burial in the cemeteries which until that collapse provide some of the best evidence for the city's continued existence.[3]

IV

If this view can be maintained, it emphasizes that the explanation of urban change in Winchester is closely related to change in function imposed by external requirements. The long period on which Winchester now enters, covering at least four centuries, from the fifth to the ninth, is both initiated and terminated by such a response to external process; in the one case, the economic and social dislocation attendant on the end of empire; in the other, the growing productive capability and consequently enhanced internal and external trade of the emerging English kingdoms.

During this long period Winchester was not an urban place, if the essential elements of urbanism include the presence of a relatively large and concentrated population engaged in

Phases (British Archaeological Reports, British Series 101, Oxford, 1982), pp. 146–56, esp. p. 153.

[1] J. P. Wild, 'The *Gynaeceum* at *Venta* and its Context', *Latomus*, 26 (1967), 648–76, concludes that of the three possibilities 'Winchester on the face of it appears to be the best choice for the site of the *gynaeceum*' (p. 676). W. H. Manning in *Antiquity*, 40 (1966), 60–2 argued that Caistor-by-Norwich (*Venta Icenorum*) could not be excluded. Cf. Sheppard Frere, *Britannia* (London, 1967), p. 300, and Peter Salway, *Roman Britain* (Oxford, 1981), p. 656.

[2] Cf., for example, the damage done to the Romano-Celtic temple in Lower Brook Street by medieval pits and foundation trenches: X. Interim, pl. L, cf. fig. 10.

[3] An abandonment never so clearly seen as in the rapid fading out of burials at the edge of the Lankhills cemetery: Winchester Studies, 3. ii, pl. ii, cf. fig. 105; see here Pl. 12*b*.

industrial and commercial activities which set it off from the surrounding countryside.

I have long argued, however, that the former city remained of considerable importance throughout this period as a centre from which authority was traditionally exercised.[1] The authority hypothesis was developed from the work of Carl-Richard Brühl on the Gallic *civitates*[2] and was a response to the need to produce a coherent explanation of the focal role apparently played by former Romano-British towns far into the early Middle Ages.[3] In the case of Winchester, the need was to find a general theory which would explain the relative concentration of sixth-century pagan Anglo-Saxon cemeteries around the city as well as the selection of Winchester in the seventh century as the site of a bishopric. The development of the argument need not be gone into again. The basic suggestion is that authority over the late Roman town, together with its *territorium* and perhaps a large part of its *civitas*, passed into the hands of those who had been entrusted with its defence. In whatever ways this group was formed and modified by external influences—and there is no space here to deal with the complex interaction of British and Germanic elements in the rise of Wessex[4]—it exercised its authority from the original seat of that authority in the former *civitas* capital, and more precisely from a site in or adjacent to the basilica of the forum, just to the west and north of the present cathedral.[5]

Does the theory stand up? A recent attempt to refute it has nothing to put in its place other than the old view—unhelpful in

[1] First argued in Biddle, 'Archaeology and the Beginnings of English Society', in P. Clemoes and K. Hughes (eds.), *England Before the Conquest* (Cambridge, 1971), pp. 393-6, and taken further in idem, 'The Development of the Anglo-Saxon Town', in *Topografia urbana e vita cittadina nell'alto medioevo in occidente* i (Settimane di studio xxi, Spoleto, 1974), 203-30, esp. 206-12; idem, 'Winchester: the Development of an Early Capital', op. cit. in p. 326 n. 1 below, pp. 237-41; and idem, 'Towns' in Wilson (ed.), op. cit. in p. 325 n. 1 below, pp. 105-6.

[2] Carl-Richard Brühl, *Palatium und civitas*, i, *Gallien* (Cologne, 1975); idem, 'Die Stätten der Herrschaftsausübung in der frühmittelalterlichen Stadt', in *Topografia urbana e vita cittadina nell'alto medioevo in occidente*, ii, (Settimane di studio, xxi, Spoleto, 1974), 621-40.

[3] Biddle, 'Towns', in Wilson (ed.), op. cit. in p. 325 n. 1 below, pp. 103-12.

[4] Biddle, 'Hampshire and the Origins of Wessex', in G. de G. Sieveking *et al.* (eds.), *Problems in Economic and Social Archaeology* (London, 1976), pp. 323-42.

[5] For the Anglo-Saxon royal palace in Winchester, see Winchester Studies, 1, pp. 289-92; and for its site and possible antiquity, see Biddle, 'The Development of an Early Capital', op. cit. in p. 326 n. 1 below, pp. 237-40 and fig. 2. The whole question will be reviewed in Winchester Studies 4. i.

the wider context of Winchester's urban history—that the re-emergence of Winchester in the seventh century was because it 'was probably chosen as the site of the new see in accordance with the wishes of the West Saxon clergy'.[1] This statement fails to account for the concentration of pre-Christian settlements reflected in the presence of fifth- to seventh-century cemeteries near the city, and ignores the need to explain the function and functioning of a missionary see distant, *ex argumento*, from a royal residence, granted that such a residence would only be occupied intermittently as one in a series of royal estates between which the king was constantly on the move. More important, this rejection of the authority hypothesis dismisses the generalizing character of the proposition. In addition, evidence is accumulating, for example from York[2] and Lincoln,[3] for just that continued use of central administrative buildings long into the post-Roman period which the theory suggests and which Brühl's original work in Gaul found so compelling.

In Winchester the authority hypothesis can finally be tested only by excavation of the site of the Anglo-Saxon royal palace. This lies immediately west of Old Minster and is either on or beside the basilica of the Roman forum. Investigation of this key area may lie far in the future, but evidence relevant to the nature of fifth- to ninth-century Winchester may come from any site in or near the town. Germanic pottery of fifth-century date was first recorded in Winchester on the Lower Brook Street site in 1970, in the tenth year of our excavations.[4] It is worth stressing this point, for it emphasizes how valueless negative evidence can be. By 1970 there had been twenty years of excavation and recording in Winchester, yet no pagan Anglo-Saxon pottery had previously been recognized. In 1970 and 1971 it was recorded on seven sites

[1] Barbara Yorke, 'The Foundation of the Old Minster and the Status of Winchester in the Seventh and Eighth Centuries', *Proceedings of the Hampshire Field Club*, 38 (1982), 75–83.

[2] B. Hope-Taylor, *Under York Minster: Archaeological Discoveries, 1966–1971* (York, 1971); A. D. Phillips, 'Excavations at York Minster, 1967–73', *Friends of York Minster, Annual Report*, 46 (1975).

[3] M. J. Jones and B. J. J. Gilmour, 'Lincoln, Principia and Forum: a Preliminary Report', *Britannia*, 11 (1980), 61–72; B. J. J. Gilmour, 'The Anglo-Saxon Church at St Paul-in-the-Bail, Lincoln', *Medieval Archaeology*, 23 (1979), 214–18. The Roman forum and the seventh-century church have been brought together in a striking diagrammatic reconstruction by Warwick Rodwell, *The Archaeology of the English Church* (London, 1981), p. 144, fig. 69, which shows that the church was constructed in the forum courtyard in a formal architectural relationship to the surrounding colonnade.

[4] IX. Interim, pp. 101–2, fig. 3.

scattered all over the walled area and has since been found in the suburbs.[1]

While some of this pottery is certainly of fifth-century date, the majority probably belongs to the sixth century or later.[2] Its discovery[3] at several different points in the city probably indicates the location of a number of discrete settlement areas of this date, the high social status of which is indicated by the residence excavated in Lower Brook Street in 1971.[4] An early stage was marked by a small cemetery, one burial in which contained a necklace with gold and garnet pendants and a collar of silver rings.[5] At a later stage this complex included timber buildings, a stone building, perhaps of two storeys (Pl. 15a), and evidence for the assaying and working of gold and for bone working.[6] At present I would see such complexes as residential enclosures of thegn-status scattered here and there in the walled area, comparable in all essentials to the postulated royal residence, and perhaps only occupied intermittently by their owners, probably when the king was also in residence in the city.

The threads of continuity between Roman *Venta* and Anglo-Saxon Winchester can thus with some degree of probability be explained by the continuing exercise of authority from a traditional centre. With the advent of Christianity in the mid seventh century these threads become clearer, but the archaeological evidence continues with increasing precision to indicate that they stretch

[1] X. Interim, pp. 117, 303, 326. Study of the pottery from the excavations of 1961–71 has subsequently shown that grass- or chaff-tempered pottery, some with distinctive early Anglo-Saxon decorative features, occurs in small quantities on most of the sites. Mr K. Qualmann tells me that it has since been found during rescue excavations in the suburbs.

[2] Dr. Helena Hamerow has examined the decorated sherds and Miss Katherine Barclay the grass-tempered material. I am grateful to them for their comments which will be pbulished in Winchester Studies, 7.i, forthcoming.

[3] In the previously published version of this paper reference was made to 'imported glass of the fifth to seventh centuries'. Re-examination of this material has shown that some if not most of this glass could equally well be of late Roman date. The whole problem will be discussed in the light of scientific analyses in Winchester Studies, 3.i, forthcoming.

[4] X. Interim, pp. 303–10. Other units of this kind are probably indicated by Ealhswith's estate (see below, p. 325 and n. 3) and by the place-name *Coiteburi* (see Winchester Studies, 1, p. 236), to the south and north of the eastern end of High Street respectively.

[5] Ibid., pp. 303–5, fig. 13; see also Sonia Chadwick Hawkes in Winchester Studies, 7. ii, forthcoming.

[6] X. Interim, p. 309; for the gold and bone working, see Winchester Studies, 7. ii, forthcoming.

back into the days when *Venta* was a centre of regional administration in Roman Britain.

V

This long period was brought to an end in the ninth century by a new movement of urban foundation in Wessex.[1] One of the major results of the excavations of 1961–71 was to show that the street plan of medieval Winchester was created in a single action at some time in the late ninth century and certainly before 901–3 when some of the streets were used as boundaries in defining the site of New Minster at the time of its foundation.[2]

Of the four elements of which the street plan is composed (Fig. 4)—High Street, the back streets flanking High Street to either side, the north–south streets, and the wall or intramural street which runs round immediately inside the city wall—two are used in the New Minster bounds: north–south streets and the back street south of High Street. The other two elements appear for the first time in the bounds of Ealhswith's tenement, which became the site of Nunnaminster. These bounds, which are no later than Ealhswith's death in 902, refer specifically to *ceapstræt* (High Street), and in mentioning the two double fords (i.e. four fords) on the course of the boundary from north to south just inside the east wall of the city imply the existence of the wall street by this date.[3]

The wall street brought the street layout and the defensive circuit into an integrated system, exactly in the manner of Roman military planning, allowing the defenders to concentrate quickly using interior lines at any threatened point of the defences. The date of the refurbishing of the defences should therefore be that of the laying out of the new street system; the streets should at least be no older. On this basis the street system has been dated to the years

[1] Biddle, 'Towns', in David M. Wilson (ed.), *The Archaeology of Anglo-Saxon England* (London, 1976), pp. 124–34.

[2] P. H. Sawyer, *Anglo-Saxon Charters: an Annotated List and Bibliography* (London, 1968), no. 1443. For a new edition, see Winchester Studies, 4. iii, no. ii. The significance of this charter for the topography and date of the Winchester street plan has been recognized since Martin Biddle and David Hill, 'Late Saxon Planned Towns', *Antiquaries Journal*, 51 (1971), 76, but the information could not be fully utilized until it was realized that the streets used as bounds could be identified with now vanished streets which formed part of the original street plan in the south-eastern quarter of the city (see Winchester Studies, 1, p. 278 n. 1). The matter will be fully discussed in Winchester Studies, 4. i.

[3] Sawyer 1560. For a new edition, see Winchester Studies, 4. iii, no. i and discussion ibid. 4. i.

between *c*.880 and 886, that is, to the period after the Battle of Edington and before the 'restoration' of London.[1] This has seemed the latest probable date on the evidence of the Winchester charters, and it cannot be much earlier if it is dependent on the assumption that the defences of Winchester were restored by Alfred as part of his 'burghal system' in the years before 892.[2]

We may well ask whether that was a fair assumption, and for an answer can look to the relationship between Winchester and Southampton in the middle years of the ninth century. During the eighth and earlier part of the ninth century Hamwic was a thriving commercial and industrial centre. Winchester during this period was something very different, not an urban place, but rather a traditional and ceremonial centre, seat of a bishop, occasional, perhaps seasonal, residence of itinerant Wessex kings.[3] By the end of the ninth century, Hamwic was virtually abandoned and Winchester once again an urban place. In the chronology of this reversal may lie the key to urban change in ninth-century Wessex.

The decline of Hamwic may have begun before the middle of the ninth century, perhaps even before the Viking raids on the settlement in 840 and 842.[4] There seems no good reason to suppose, however, that the commercial needs fulfilled by Hamwic disappeared, least of all in the period following Egbert's (802-39) great expansion of the power of Wessex, consolidated by his son Æthelwulf (839-55).[5] Wider European movements may have led to a decrease in international trade,[6] but manufacture and internal trade will not have ceased.

If we now turn to Winchester, we see perhaps the other side of this coin. In 859, according to a tenth-century poem, Bishop

[1] For successive stages in the refinement of this date, see II. Interim, pp. 215–17; III. Interim, p. 242; Biddle and Hill, op. cit. in p. 325 n. 2 above, pp. 70–85, esp. pp. 76–8; Biddle, 'Winchester: the Development of an Early Capital', in H. Jankuhn *et al.* (eds.), *Vor- und Frühformen der europäischen Stadt im Mittelalter*, i (Göttingen, 1973), 229–61, esp. 248–50; and Winchester Studies, i, p. 273, esp. n. 7, and pp. 277–9.

[2] F. M. Stenton, *Anglo-Saxon England* (3rd edn., Oxford, 1971), pp. 264–5.

[3] For the characterization of this relationship, see Biddle, 'Winchester: the Development of an Early Capital', op. cit. in n. 1 above, pp. 242–7.

[4] John F. Cherry and Richard Hodges, 'The Dating of Hamwih: Saxon Southampton Reconsidered', *Antiquaries Journal*, 58 (1978), 299–309. Mr Mark Brisbane (pers. comm.) tells me that he would now put the beginning of the decline in the 840s with virtual abandonment by 880.

[5] Stenton, op. cit. in n. 2 above, pp. 232–5, 244–5.

[6] For a recent view, see Richard Hodges and David Whitehouse, *Mohammed, Charlemagne and the Origins of Europe* (London, 1983), pp. 158–68.

Swithun (852–62) built a bridge over the river Itchen, immediately outside East Gate.[1] The road which led over this bridge was the principal, possibly at this time the only, route through the walled town, and by 902 at the latest it was the *ceapstræt* of the city. But the blocking of South Gate (Pl. 16) had already ensured as early as the sixth or seventh century that all through traffic would follow this east–west line.[2] Swithun's reported action in providing a permanent bridge to carry this road over the Itchen may thus suggest that traffic had increased to such an extent on the approach to Winchester that a bridge had become an urgent requirement. A year later in 860 Winchester was stormed by the Vikings.[3]

It was during the reign of Æthelbald (855–60) that the triple duty of service in the army, bridge building, and fortress construction was first regularly reserved in the diplomas of a king of Wessex.[4] This does not mean that these burdens were not owed before his reign, nor does their reservation under Æthelbald necessarily mean that this king levied these duties to a greater extent than his predecessors, although it must indicate his concern that they should be leviable when needed and not eroded in their yield.

Hamwic seems never to have had defences, although the 1982 excavations at Six Dials showed that the area of intense settlement was defined to the west by a boundary ditch of less than defensive scale.[5] Winchester on the other hand lay within its Roman wall, and the blocking of South Gate by a cross-ditch in the sixth or seventh century, replaced by a stone blocking *c.*700 (Pl. 16), shows that the Roman wall had remained an effective barrier, even if it was not defensible. Swithun's probable construction of the

---

[1] Winchester Studies, 1, pp. 271–2. For a new edition of the poem, see Winchester Studies, 4. ii. In the late eleventh century the bridge was *arcubus lapideis opere non leviter ruituro* (E. P. Sauvage, *Analecta Bollandiana*, 7 (1888), 378, ll. 16–18). Whether this stone bridge was the same as the one said by the poem to have been built by Swithun, and described there simply as *operatio pulchra*, is unknown.

[2] X. Interim, pp. 117–18; cf. Winchester Studies, 1, pp. 261–3, 276, 278.

[3] C. Plummer (ed.), *Two of the Saxon Chronicles Parallel*, i (Oxford, rev. imp. 1965), 67–8.

[4] Nicholas Brooks, 'The Development of Military Obligations in Eighth- and Ninth-Century England', in P. Clemoes and K. Hughes (eds.), *England Before the Conquest. Studies in Primary Sources Presented to Dorothy Whitelock* (Cambridge, 1971), pp. 69–84, esp. pp. 81–2.

[5] I am indebted to Mr Mark Brisbane for showing me his excavations at Six Dials and for discussing many points of Hamwic archaeology in advance of publication.

Itchen bridge at East Gate in 859 may well reflect a period of renewed attention to the defences at just the time when Æthelbald was first reserving, presumably under the threat of Viking attack, the triple duty of bridge work, fortification, and army service. The use of the word *abræcan* in the annal for 860,[1] describing the Viking attack on Winchester, implies that there were defences to be breached, and although we cannot necessarily assume that these were other than the decayed Roman wall, it looks as if this had to be forced and was thus defended. It may also be of some significance that Æthelweard in recording this event describes Winchester as *urbs regia*, a phrase not found in the Chronicle.[2]

If the urban revival of Winchester belongs to the 880s, there seems to be an uncomfortable gap opening in the provision of urban functions in Wessex between the decline of Hamwic and the rise of Winchester. The extraordinary wealth of Hamwic, its considerable population, and the services of exchange and production which it provided, cannot in the general context of the advance of Wessex in the ninth century have vanished. They can only have moved elsewhere. If, however, it was Æthelbald who started the process of re-urbanization at Winchester (perhaps with the collaboration of Swithun whose concern for his episcopal city was often recalled in later years),[3] the shift from the undefended port to the walled city may have been one continuous process.

This suggestion would allow the laying of the new grid of streets to either side of High Street, together with the wall street, to be dated earlier than *c*.880-6. This would fit better with the evidence for the high value of inherited land in the centre of the city which had to be purchased by Edward the Elder in 901-3 for the site of New Minster from those *circummanentibus iure haereditatis*,[4] but it is still impossible on archaeological grounds alone to date the use of the earliest excavated streets more accurately than to *c*.900 with a considerable margin of error.[5] One should always remember that

[1] Plummer, loc. cit. in p. 327 n. 3 above. Æthelweard used *fregerunt*: A. Campbell (ed.), *The Chronicle of Æthelweard* (London, 1962), p. 35. *brecan, abrecan* is the normal Old English word used in the Chronicle for successful attacks on *fortified* places: see, for example, Canterbury and London (s.a. 851 ADE, 853 C), York (s.a. 867 ADE, 868 C), the unfinished fortification, ? Newenden, Kent (s.a. 892 AE, 893 CD; cf. B. K. Davison in *Medieval Archaeology*, 16 (1972), 123-7); Benfleet (s.a. 893 AE, 894 CD).

[2] Campbell (ed.), loc. cit. in n. 1 above, p. 35.

[3] For the historical Swithun and his cult, see Winchester Studies, 4. ii.

[4] Winchester Studies, 1, p. 314.

[5] Gar Street (III. Interim, p. 242); north-south street below the castle (VIII. Interim, pp. 285-9; for an uncalibrated radiocarbon date of a.d. 880 ± 60

the laying out of the streets not only organized the interior space in relation to the defences, but also reflects the division and apportionment of the area for permanent settlement. Whether in Winchester this definitive act should still be regarded as belonging to the 880s, whether indeed it is Alfredian at all, rather than the work of one of his elder brothers, must be a matter for future investigation.

The dating of the beginning of the decline of Hamwic to the 840s, and the possibility that the urban revival of Winchester began earlier than c.880-6 (even if only in an initial stage expressed mainly in the refurbishing of the defences), appear to fit very well the postulated existence of a mint at Southampton until early in the reign of Æthelwulf (839–58), followed by break in the operation of a mint or mints in Wessex until the opening of the Winchester mint at the very end of the century.[1]

The sequence suggested here may also bear on another problem: the source of the population of the renewed urban community in Winchester. For if the shift from Hamwic to Winchester was a continuous process, it seems reasonable to suppose that some at least of the new Wintonians had previously been among the 5,000 or so inhabitants of Hamwic.[2] Nor, apparently, did all the newcomers settle within the walls. The evidence for occupation as early as the late ninth century in the western suburb of Winchester, along Sussex Street to the north of West Gate, is striking and requires further investigation.[3] What the attraction of extramural living might be at just the moment when defence must have seemed the paramount concern is not obvious. What advantages can an extramural tenement have enjoyed that were

(calibrated AD 902±60) for material on the lowest surface of this street, see X. Interim, p. 103); wall-street below the castle (X. Interim, p. 103).

[1] Michael Dolley, 'The Location of the pre-Ælfredian Mint(s) of Wessex', *Proceedings of the Hampshire Field Club*, 27 (1970), 57–61.

[2] The figure is based on the density of buildings on the Six Dials site which suggests a population of c. 200 persons to the hectare or c. 9,000 for the c. 45-hectare settlement as a whole. Since all sites so far examined seem to show the same density of features, this seems a reasonable extrapolation, but it has been halved to allow for possible variations in population density over the area as a whole. I am grateful to Mr Mark Brisbane for this information: the halving is my responsibility.

[3] David A. Hinton, Suzanne Keene, and Kenneth E. Qualmann, 'The Winchester Reliquary', *Medieval Archaeology*, 25 (1981), 48–9. If the refurbishing of the defences is to be dated earlier than c.880-6, as suggested here, the Sussex Street occupation, which overlies what may be upcast from the newly dug ditch system, may also be dated earlier than was previously thought. This would seem to be quite consistent with the evidence of the pottery.

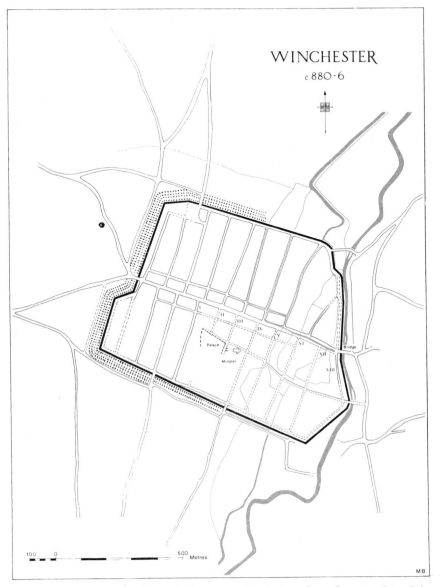

FIG. 4. Winchester in the later ninth century. Revised to show the extension of the
northern back street west to the wall street (discovered in 1984 at Staple Gardens), and
the stretch of the southern back street between II and III (found in 1988 at 31 A–B,
The Square).

denied to someone who dwelt within the walls? It cannot be
irrelevant to this enquiry that the western suburb formed an
important part of the king's fief in Winchester, and by 1148 was
(next to High Street) the most intensively developed area of the
city and showed signs that this development had been in progress
for a long time.[1]

[1] Winchester Studies, 1, pp. 350–1, 380–1, 453.

To turn lastly to one specific aspect of Winchester's ninth-century urban renewal: the street plan itself. Not all scholars have accepted that the regular arrangement of the streets (Fig. 4) is necessarily the result of deliberate planning. Some have preferred rather to regard the regularity as the inevitable result of laying out properties to either side of the pre-existing axis of High Street, and within the rectangular frame provided by the Roman defences.[1] To my mind there have so far been three substantial arguments in favour of deliberate planning: first, the similarity in construction of the first street surface wherever it has been seen in Winchester;[2] second, the use of plans of 'Winchester type', involving the same components of axial street, back streets, side streets, and wall streets, in a series of other burhs, many of them on new sites; and third, the predictability of the pattern in Winchester itself. This predictability allowed one to suggest the original layout over much of the south-eastern quarter of the city, where it was subsequently lost by the creation and extension of the sites of the three minsters and the royal palace, but where it has now been shown to have existed (Fig. 4), both by excavation and by fresh topographical analysis, especially of the relevant Anglo-Saxon charters.[3]

The reality of deliberate planning (and the reason for the predictability of the system where it had vanished) has now received strong support from Philip Crummy's analysis of the layout of the street systems of parts of Colchester and London, and that of Winchester itself.[4] He has effectively demonstrated that the

[1] Hinton, *Alfred's Kingdom: Wessex and the South 800–1500* (London, 1977), pp. 60–5, accepts that the Winchester plan was 'new, an act of deliberate creation' (p. 61), but seems to regard other plans of the same type as more probably the result of piecemeal growth conditioned by rectilinear defences and the position of gates, whether of Roman or 'Alfredian' date. See also Helen Clarke, reviewing Winchester Studies 1, in the *Bulletin of the Institute of Archaeology of the University of London*, 15 (1978), 255.

[2] VIII. Interim, p. 287; X. Interim, p. 103; Winchester Studies, 1, p. 450.

[3] Winchester Studies, 1, p. 278 n. 1. The matter will be discussed in detail in Winchester Studies, 4. i.

[4] Philip Crummy, 'The System of Measurement used in Town Planning from the Ninth to the Thirteenth Centuries', *Anglo-Saxon Studies in Archaeology and History*, 1 (1979) [= British Archaeological Reports, British Series, 72], 149–64; idem, 'Colchester Between the Roman and Norman Conquests', in D. G. Buckley (ed.), *Archaeology in Essex to AD 1500* (Council for British Archaeology, Research Report 34, London, 1980), pp. 76–81; and idem, *Aspects of Anglo-Saxon and Norman Colchester* (Council for British Archaeology, Research Report 39, London, 1981), pp. 50–1, 71–4. Crummy has suggested in these papers that the Winchester street plan may be earlier than the 880s. He

module used was a 4-pole unit (4 × 16½ feet) of 66 feet or 1 chain, now enshrined in English hearts as the length of a cricket pitch, but already used in seventh-century Winchester for the length of the original nave of Old Minster. This demonstration of conscious order underlying the regularity of the street systems of pre-Conquest England provides not only a powerful proof that they were deliberately planned, but also an insight which may well be called archaeological into the minds of Anglo-Saxon men.[1]

VI

This is as far as I intend to go on this occasion in reviewing current knowledge of the development of early Winchester. Similar re-evaluations are taking place in the other phases of Winchester's past, in the long second cycle of urbanization from the tenth to the fifteenth century,[2] in the crisis of the sixteenth and seventeenth centuries, and in the third cycle which sees the emergence of the county town from the later seventeenth century onwards.[3] My purpose here has been to show something of the kind of work and rethinking which is possible when the evidential base is broad and full of detail.

If I have concentrated on the urban phenomenon and its change through time, that is because it was the theme with which our work at Winchester began twenty-two years ago, and because in a paper such as this one can only offer an adequate discussion of a few themes. This emphasis on the urban phenomenon, on aspects of social and cultural archaeology, should not obscure the broader character of the work of the Excavations Committee and the Research Unit, much of which has been concerned with

also suggests, however, that it might be as early as the period immediately after the Viking raid of 860 (see above, p. 327) and was possible because of the supposed extent of the devastation on that occasion. There is, I think, as yet no good evidence for dating the street plan so early, and no evidence at all for any devastation in the mid ninth century. The laying out of the street plan over virtually the whole of the walled area was possible in the later ninth century, not because the town was cleared by fire or otherwise devastated, but because the walled area was then to a great extent not built up due to the special character of early medieval Winchester up to this time as a ceremonial and ecclesiastical centre (cf. Biddle, 'Winchester: the Development of an Early Capital', op. cit. in p. 326 n. 1 above, pp. 239–49).

[1] Colin Renfrew, *Towards an Archaeology of Mind* (Inaugural Lecture, Cambridge, 1982), p. 21.

[2] See now especially the *Survey of Medieval Winchester* by Derek Keene (Winchester Studies 2, Oxford, 1984).

[3] Rosen, op. cit. in p. 319 n. 5 above.

buildings, with architectural archaeology, and with the attempt to put back into architectural history, as well as into the evolving fabric of Winchester, the great creations of the built past such as the Old Minster, Wolvesey, and Winchester Castle, or the lesser houses and churches which composed the foil to these greater structures across the wider part of the city. There are many archaeologies, of art, of architecture, of culture, society, and mind, and the house of archaeology is large enough to contain them all.

The lessons learnt and the needs now

This attempt to explain some of the premises which lay behind our work in Winchester, and to illustrate our approach by a consideration of a few of the larger problems, should not end without some statement of the general lessons learnt and the principal needs for the future.

First, is the absolute importance of general and specific model building, or if you wish hypothesis formation. Without such hypotheses our work would have been without form and direction from the start. Thus, while I would not accept Hugh Thompson's view that much of urban rescue archaeology can be characterized as rubbish collection rather than research,[1] urban archaeology without the direction provided by the formation and testing of hypotheses results in mere data collection. It is because simple hypotheses about the development of Winchester in general and aspects of its fabric in particular—such as the roles played by Old Minster or Wolvesey Palace, and the interrelation of the various components of the city across the social classes—guided our work from the beginning, that the 2 per cent of the walled area which we excavated can be relied upon in further theory building to a greater extent than such a small proportion of the walled area might otherwise allow.

Second, one must stress the need for quantification and conceptual interpretation if we are to proceed to the next stage of comparative studies, and eventually to explanation. It is an irony of our knowledge of eleventh- and twelfth-century Winchester that precisely because it is so detailed, it is difficult to evaluate, for there is little with which to compare it.

Only in a few fields, notably in the study of the mint, are we yet able to evaluate the status of Winchester in relation to other towns. Without such comparison we cannot accurately understand the role and character of the city itself.

[1]See above, p. 302 n. 4.

The concept of functional change which I have stressed in this lecture may also be useful in comparative studies, not only between one town and another, but also diachronically within a single town (as between Roman and early modern Winchester) and cross-culturally between different societies (as between trading places or ceremonial centres in different cultures). Diachronic and cross-cultural studies demand, however, accurate chronological definition and scrupulous cultural description. Without a body of data which is well-founded and sufficiently extensive to carry the weight of such definition and description, diachronic and cross-cultural comparisons and all attempts at the explanation of cultural process must fail. I hope to have shown in this paper that the establishment of an adequate body of data comes only with long-continued investment which builds on strength and which operates on a scale commensurate with the opportunities offered and above all with the questions being asked. There is, unfortunately, rarely any point in small-scale excavations on urban sites.

My third point is that one cannot in urban archaeology separate research objectives and their achievement from the practical considerations of working within the pressures of a living town. Never was research conducted further from an ivory tower. These considerations almost inevitably involve high costs which have led some to question the heavy expenditure on urban archaeology by comparison with other areas of archaeological activity. I hope to have shown, however, that even in a town where much has been spent, with reasonably well-defined objectives, as much or even more remains to be learnt, principally because we can now define more closely what the real problems are, where the gaps in our knowledge lie, and what we must do to fill them. It is precisely the long continuance of work in Winchester which is yielding results that are more than superficial sketches of the city's development and changing character. Only the further continuation of work in Winchester, York, Southampton, Lincoln, London, Canterbury, and other cities large and small will eventually teach us something worth knowing about the development of the British town. The archaeology of a town must be backed with long-continued resources if the value of an initial investment is to be realized to the full. It is also too important to be left to rescue work alone. Research considerations, in urban as in other archaeology, should be the guide to future work.

Lastly, one must stress that a long-term archaeological presence is necessary in our major towns for the foreseeable future. The sudden introduction of outside teams into the complex research framework of a town's archaeology is intellectually and financially ineffective. The kind of technician's archaeology now on the increase, competent but conducted without understanding of the problems involved, is no answer to the problems of archaeology in British towns, or indeed of British archaeology. The role of local authorities in supporting active, continuing, professional archaeology in our towns is essential. It may also perhaps offer the best hope that research objectives rather than rescue requirements may come to dominate the field. An informed local authority is, after all, more likely to be concerned with the excitement and value of knowledge about its town than simply with the need to rescue sites before they are destroyed.

It is the good fortune of Winchester that it has for long had such a local authority, whose good will was the basis of our work and ensured for us so much support and not least that of this Academy.

Felix urbs Winthonia

Acknowledgements: I am most grateful to colleagues who have helped in the preparation of this paper, especially Katherine Barclay, Mark Brisbane, Birthe Kjølbye-Biddle, and Kenneth Qualmann, but they should not be held responsible for the opinions it contains and any errors which may remain. The line-drawings and photographs are the copyright of the Winchester Excavations Committee.

The work at Winchester since 1961 would not have been possible without the generous financial support of the Department of the Environment, the Hampshire County Council, the Winchester City Council, and many other public and private bodies: The American Council of Learned Societies (USA), The Avenue Trust, Barclays Bank, The Mary Duke Biddle Foundation (USA), The British Academy, the British Museum, The Calouste Gulbenkian Foundation, Duke University (USA), The Grocer's Charitable Trust, The Haverfield Trust, The Robert Kiln Charitable Trust, the Leverhulme Trust, The National Endowment for the Humanities (USA), The Nuffield Trust, The Old Dominion Foundation (USA), The Pilgrim Trust, The Rank Foundation, The Jean Sainsbury Charitable Trust, The Social Science Research Council, The Society of Antiquaries of London, The University of North Carolina (USA), The Fellows of Winchester College, The Wolfson Foundation, and many private donors. The Hayward Foundation has provided the subsidy needed for the publication of Winchester Studies.

APPENDIX A

Interim reports on the excavations of 1961–71 were published annually.
The short titles shown here are used in the footnotes to the present article
and in Winchester Studies.

I. Interim   Martin Biddle and R. N. Quirk, 'Excavations near
       Winchester Cathedral, 1961', *Archaeological Journal*, 119
       (1962), 150–94, with appendices on the documentary
       evidence relating to the three Saxon minsters and on
       selected finds.

II. Interim   Martin Biddle, 'Excavations at Winchester 1962–63,
       Second Interim Report', *Antiquaries Journal*, 44 (1964),
       188–219, with an appendix on 'Guenta' by Frank
       Barlow, pp. 217–19.

III. Interim   Idem, 'Excavations at Winchester 1964, Third Interim
       Report', ibid. 45 (1965), 230–64, with an appendix on
       'Late Saxon Metalwork from the Old Minster, 1964',
       by David M. Wilson, pp. 262–4.

IV. Interim   Idem, 'Excavations at Winchester 1965, Fourth Interim
       Report', ibid. 46 (1966), 308–32, with an appendix on
       'A Late Saxon Frieze Sculpture from the Old Minster',
       by Martin Biddle, pp. 329–32.

V. Interim   Idem, 'Excavations at Winchester 1966, Fifth Interim
       Report', ibid. 47 (1967), 251–79, with an appendix on
       'A Late Ninth-century Wall Painting from the Site of
       New Minster', by Martin Biddle, pp. 277–9; see also
       Francis Wormald, ibid. pp. 162–5.

VI. Interim   Idem, 'Excavations at Winchester 1967, Sixth Interim
       Report', ibid. 48 (1968), 250–84.

VII. Interim   Idem, 'Excavations at Winchester 1968, Seventh
       Interim Report', ibid. 49 (1969), 295–328, with an
       appendix on 'A Late Anglo-Saxon Strap-end', by
       David M. Wilson, pp. 326–8.

VIII. Interim Idem, 'Excavations at Winchester 1969, Eighth Interim
       Report', ibid. 50 (1970), 277–326.

IX. Interim   Idem, 'Excavations at Winchester 1970, Ninth Interim
       Report', ibid. 52 (1972), 93–131.

X. Interim   Idem, 'Excavations at Winchester 1971, Tenth Interim
       Report', ibid. 55 (1975), 96–126, 295–337, with an
       appendix on 'A Wooden Statuette from *Venta Belgarum*',
       by Anne Ross, pp. 335–6.

APPENDIX B

The final reports on the excavations of 1961–71 are appearing, together with the results of allied research carried out by the Winchester Research Unit, in a series entitled 'Winchester Studies' which is being published at the Clarendon Press, Oxford. The excavations of 1949–60 and those carried out since 1972 are being published in two series entitled *Winchester Excavations 1949–60* and *Winchester Excavations since 1972*, for which see above, p. 300 n. 4 and p. 309 n. 2.

The list of Winchester Studies which follows has been revised up to 1984. Volumes 1, 2, and 3. ii have already been published.

WINCHESTER STUDIES

1 *Winchester in the Early Middle Ages: an Edition and Discussion of the Winton Domesday*, by Frank Barlow, Martin Biddle, Olof von Feilitzen, and D. J. Keene, with contributions by T. J. Brown, H. M. Nixon, and Francis Wormald (published January 1976), xxxiv. 612.

2 *Survey of Medieval Winchester* (in two parts) by D. J. Keene, with a contribution by Alexander R. Rumble (published December 1985), xxxviii. 1490.

3 *Pre-Roman and Roman Winchester*:

    Part I   *Venta Belgarum*, by Martin Biddle and others, and including a gazetteer of pre-Roman and Roman discoveries by Kenneth Qualmann.

    Part II   *The Roman Cemetery at Lankhills*, by Giles Clarke with contributions by J. L. Macdonald and others (published January 1980), xlii. 468.

4 *The Anglo-Saxon Minsters of Winchester*:

    Part I   *The Anglo-Saxon Minsters*, by Martin Biddle, Birthe Kjølbye-Biddle, and others, and including a gazetteer of early and middle Saxon discoveries and of all other discoveries from the area of the Close by Kenneth Qualmann.

    Part II   *The Cult of St. Swithun*, by Michael Lapidge, with contributions by Robert Deshman and Susan Rankine.

    Part III   *Anglo-Saxon and Early Norman Charters Relating to the Topography of Winchester*, by Alexander R. Rumble.

5 *The Brooks and Other Town Sites of Medieval Winchester*, by Martin Biddle and others, including a gazetteer of late Saxon and medieval discoveries, other than from the Close, by Kenneth Qualmann, and

an analysis of the radiocarbon and dendrochronology dating project by R. Otlet and A. C. Barefoot.

6 *Winchester Castle and Wolvesey Palace*:

Part I   *Winchester Castle*, by Martin Biddle and Beatrice Clayre.

Part II   *Wolvesey Palace*, by Martin Biddle and Henri Galinié.

7 *The Crafts and Industries of Medieval Winchester*:

Part I   *The Pottery of Medieval Winchester*, by Katherine Barclay and others.

Part II   *The Arts, Crafts, Industries, and Daily Life of Medieval Winchester*, by Martin Biddle and others (published 1989).

8 *The Winchester Mint and Other Medieval Numismatic Studies*, by Yvonne Harvey and others, edited by Martin Biddle.

9 *Human and Animal Biology*:

Part I   *The People of Early Winchester*, by D. R. Brothwell, Theya Molleson, and Caroline Stuckert.

Part II   *The Animals of Early Winchester*, by Pauline Sheppard, Gina Adams, and others.

10 *The Environment, Agriculture, and Gardens in Early Winchester*, edited by Jane M. Renfrew, with contributions by F. Green, M. Monk, P. R. Murphy, J. Z. Titow, and others.

11 *The Origins and Development of Winchester: a General Survey*, by Martin Biddle, including a bibliography of writing on Winchester and a general index.

APPENDIX C

A selective bibliography of articles on, preparatory to, or resulting from, the excavations of 1961–71, the work of the Winchester Research Unit since 1968, and the activity of the Winchester City Archaeologist since 1972. For interim reports 1961–71, see Appendix A. For interim reports since 1972, see *Find* (the Newsletter of the Winchester Archaeological Rescue Group). For final reports 1949–60, 1961–71, and 1972 onwards, see Appendix B.

Barefoot, A. C., Woodhouse, Lewis B., Hafley, William L., and Wilson, E. H., 'Developing a Dendrochronology for Winchester, England', *Journal of the Institute of Wood Science*, 6 (5) (June 1974), 34–40.
—— 'A Winchester Dendrochronology for 1635–1972 AD: its Validity and Possible Extension', ibid. 7 (1) (May 1975), 25–32.
—— Hafley, W. L., and Hughes, J. F., 'Dendrochronology and the Winchester Excavation', in Fletcher, J. (ed.), *Dendrochronology in*

Europe (British Archaeological Reports, International Series 51, Oxford, 1978), pp. 162-72.

Biddle, Martin, 'Winchester: the Archaeology of a City', *Science Journal* I (i) (March 1965), 55-61.

—— 'Health in Medieval Winchester: the Evidence from Excavations', in Cockburn, Aidan (ed.), *Infectious Diseases: their Evolution and Eradication* (Springfield, Illinois, 1967), pp. 58-60.

—— 'Two Burials of the First Century AD from Winchester', *Antiquaries Journal*, 47 (1967), 224-50.

—— 'Wolvesey: the *domus quasi palatium* of Henry de Blois in Winchester', *Château Gaillard*, 3 (1969), 28-36.

—— 'Winchester 1961-68', ibid. 4 (1969), 19-30.

—— 'Winchester: the Development of an Early Capital', in Jankuhn, H., Schlesinger, W., and Steuer, H. (eds.), *Vor- und Frühformen der europäischen Stadt im Mittelalter*, i (Abhandlungen der Akademie der Wissenschaften, Philologisch-Historische Klasse, 3te Folge, Nr. 83, Göttingen, 1973), 229-61.

—— 'The Archaeology of Winchester', *Scientific American* (May 1974), pp. 32-43.

—— 'The Evolution of Towns: Planned Towns before 1066', in Barley, M. W. (ed.), *The Plans and Topography of Medieval Towns in England and Wales* (Council for British Archaeology, Research Report 14, London, 1975), pp. 19-32.

—— 'Ptolemaic Coins from Winchester', *Antiquity*, 49 (1975), 213-15.

—— 'Felix urbs Winthonia: Winchester in the Age of Monastic Reform', in Parsons, D. (ed.), *Tenth-century Studies* (Chichester and London, 1975), pp. 123-40.

—— 'Venta Belgarum (Winchester)', in Stillwell, Richard (ed.), *The Princeton Encyclopedia of Classical Sites* (Princeton, 1976), pp. 964-5.

—— 'Hampshire and the Origins of Wessex', in Sieveking, G. de G., Longworth, I. H., and Wilson, K. E. (eds.), *Problems in Economic and Social Archaeology* (London, 1976), pp. 323-42.

—— *Wolvesey: the Old Bishop's Palace* (English Heritage, London, 1986).

—— *King Arthur's Round Table: an Archaeological Investigation* (London, 1989).

—— 'Archaeology, Architecture, and the Cult of Saints in Anglo-Saxon England', in Butler, L. A. S., and Morris, R. K. (eds.), *The Anglo-Saxon Church. Papers on History, Architecture, and Archaeology in Honour of Dr. H. M. Taylor* (Council for British Archaeology Research Report 60, London, 1986), pp. 1-31.

—— 'Seasonal Festivals and Residence: Winchester, Westminster and Gloucester in the Tenth to Twelfth Centuries', *Anglo-Norman Studies* 8 (1986), 51-72.

——'Early Norman Winchester', in Holt, J. C. (ed.), *Domesday Studies* (Woodbridge, 1987), pp. 311–31.

——'Winchester: The Rise of an Early Capital', in Ford, Boris (ed.), *The Cambridge Guide to the Arts in Britain* 1 (Cambridge, 1988), pp. 194–205.

——and Barclay, Katherine, 'Winchester Ware', in Evison, Vera I., Hodges, H., and Hurst, J. G. (eds.), *Medieval Pottery from Excavations: Studies Presented to Gerald Clough Dunning* (London, 1974), pp. 137–65.

——and Clayre, Beatrice, *Winchester Castle and the Great Hall* (Winchester, 1983).

——and Collis, John, 'A New Type of 9th and 10th-century Pottery from Winchester', *Medieval Archaeology*, 22 (1978), 133–5.

——and Hill, David, 'Late Saxon Planned Towns', *Antiquaries Journal*, 51 (1971), 70–85.

Biddle, Martin, and Kjølbye-Biddle, Birthe, 'Metres, Areas and Robbing', *World Archaeology*, 1 (1969), 208–19.

——*Winchester: Saxon and Norman art* (Catalogue of an exhibition in Winchester Cathedral Treasury, revised edition with illustrations, Winchester, 1973).

Collis, John and Kjølbye-Biddle, Birthe, 'Early Medieval Bone Spoons from Winchester', *Antiquaries Journal*, 59 (1979), 375–91.

Dolley, R. H. M., 'A Recent Find of Long Cross Pennies of Henry III from Winchester', *Numismatic Chronicle*, 7th ser. 1 (1961), 185–9.

Dolley, Michael and Blunt, C. E., 'Coins from the Winchester Excavations 1961–1973', *British Numismatic Journal*, 47 (1978), 135–8.

Hinton, David A., Keene, Suzanne, and Qualmann, Kenneth E., 'The Winchester Reliquary', *Medieval Archaeology*, 25 (1981), 45–77.

Keene, Derek, 'Suburban Growth', in Barley, M. W. (ed.), *The Plans and Topography of Medieval Towns in England and Wales* (Council for British Archaeology, Research Report 14, London, 1975), pp. 71–82.

——'Medieval Winchester: its Spatial Organization', in Burnham, Barry C. and Kingsbury, John (eds.), *Space, Hierarchy and Society: Interdisciplinary Studies in Social Area Analysis* (British Archaeological Reports, International Series 59, 1979), pp. 149–59.

——'Rubbish in Medieval Towns', in Hall, A. R. and Kenward, H. K. (eds.), *Environmental Archaeology in the Urban Context* (Council for British Archaeology, Research Report 43, London, 1982), pp. 26–30.

——'Town into Gown: the Site of the College and other College Lands in Winchester before the Reformation', in Custance, R. (ed.), *Winchester College Sixth-centenary Essays* (Oxford, 1982), pp. 37–75.

——'The Medieval Urban Environment in Written Records', *Archives*, 16 (1983), 137–44.

——'Introduction to the Parish Churches of Medieval Winchester', *Bulletin of the CBA Churches Committee*, 23 (Winter, 1983), 1–9.

Keene, Suzanne, 'An Approach to the Sampling and Storage of Waterlogged Timbers from Excavations', *The Conservator*, 1 (1977), 8–11.

Kjølbye-Biddle, Birthe, 'A Cathedral Cemetery: Problems in Excavation and Interpretation', *World Archaeology*, 7 (1) (1975), 87–108.

——'The Seventh-Century Minster Church at Winchester Interpreted', in Butler, L. A. S. and Morris, R. K. (eds.), *The Anglo-Saxon Church. Studies on History, Architecture, and Archaeology in Honour of Dr. H. M. Taylor* (Council for British Archaeology, Research Report 60, London, 1986) pp. 196–209.

——'The Winchester "Weather Vane" Reconsidered' in Lind, Birgit *et al.* (eds.), *Mindeskrift til Ole Klindt-Jensen* (= *Hikuin* 10 (1984)), pp. 307–14.

——and Page, R. I., 'A Scandinavian Rune Stone from Winchester', *Antiquaries Journal*, 55 (1975), 389–94.

Laurent, V., 'Byzance et l'Angleterre au lendemain de la conquête normande: à propos d'un sceau byzantin trouvé à Winchester', *Numismatic Circular*, 71 (1963), 93–6.

——'Un sceau inédit du patriarche de Jérusalem Sophrone II trouvé à Winchester', ibid. 72 (1964), 49–50.

Pike, A. W. and Biddle, Martin, 'Parasite Eggs in Medieval Winchester', *Antiquity*, 40 (1966), 293–6.

Qualmann, Kenneth E., 'Rescue Archaeology in the City of Winchester', *District Councils Review*, March 1975, 64–7.

——'A Late-Roman Cemetery at West Hill, Winchester', *Britannia*, 12 (1981), 295–7.

Quirk, R. N., 'Winchester Cathedral in the Tenth Century', *Archaeological Journal*, 114 (1957), 28–68.

——'Winchester New Minster and its Tenth-century Tower', *Journal of the British Archaeological Association*, 3rd ser. 24 (1961), 16–54.

Rance, Adrian, *A Prospect of Winchester: a Guide to the City Museum* (Winchester, 1978).

Schadla-Hall, R. T., *Winchester District: the Archaeological Potential* (Winchester, 1977).

Sheerin, D. J., 'The Dedication of the Old Minster, Winchester, in 980', *Revue Bénédictine*, 88 (1978), 261–72.

PLATE 11

Winchester Cathedral and the excavation of Old Minster, 1966.

PLATE 12

(*a*) Old Minster: the excavation in 1968 of the northern apse of the double-apsed martyrium built *c*.971–4 around the tomb of St Swithun (d. 862), looking north. Trench XXXIII, discussed on pp. 306–7, occupied the central foreground, around the tomb of Swithun.

(*b*) Lankhills: the excavation in 1972 of the eastern limit of the late Roman cemetery, looking east. See p. 321 and n. 3.

PLATE 13

(*a*) Winchester Castle: the excavation in 1968 of the early twelfth-century keep below Castle Yard, looking north-west.

(*b*) Winchester Castle: the excavation in 1971 of the early Norman chapel built *c.* 1070 using the Anglo-Saxon structural technique of long-and-short quoins, looking south-east.

PLATE 14

(a) Wolvesey from the air, 1966. The bishop's palace lies within the south-east angle of the Roman and medieval city wall, seen to the left. Looking south-west.

(b) Wolvesey: the excavation in 1971 of Henry of Blois's east hall, built c.1135–8, showing the ditches of an Anglo-Saxon field (meadow?) system running at an angle below it. Looking south-east.

PLATE 15

(b) Lower Brook Street: the excavation in 1969 of House XII, with St Pancras Lane (*centre*) and rows of flint-packed post-holes for tenter-racks on the site of House XI (*left*). Looking west.

(a) Lower Brook Street: the excavation in 1970 of the church of St Mary in Tanner Street, looking west. The church reached this form c.1000, but the nave was originally constructed c.800 as a domestic structure of stone in an estate of thegn status. (See p. 324.)

PLATE 16

South Gate: the excavation in 1971 of the Roman south gate of *Venta Belgarum*, looking north-west. The cambered Roman road (*under the right-hand scale*) has been blocked by the cutting of a ditch *under the left-hand scale*. The blocking was subsequently reinforced by the construction of a stone wall along the inner edge of the ditch. See p. 327.